Elizabeth Buchan was born in 1948 and lived in a variety of places during her childhood, including Africa. She gained an Honours Degree in English and History and began working in publishing soon after. She is married to a grandson of John Buchan and has a son and daughter. Elizabeth Buchan has also written *Ice Dancer* (1985), a role-playing adventure romance, *Beatrix Potter: A Profile* (1987), and is currently working on a historical novel set in the French Revolution.

A Dashing Young Tiger Named Jack

and Other Silly Limericks

Edited by
Elizabeth Buchan
and
Illustrated by
Scoular Anderson

A Piccolo Original

First published 1987 by Pan Books Ltd,
Cavaye Place, London SW10 9PG
9 8 7 6 5 4 3 2 1

ISBN 0 330 29630 2
Printed and bound in Great Britain by
Cox & Wyman Ltd, Reading

DEDICATION

This book is dedicated to all the doctors and nursing staff in the children's wards of St Thomas' Hospital who took care of my small daughter when she was ill.

It is also for all sick children everywhere.

Contents

A dashing young tiger named Jack
Grew up without stripes on his back.
He tried with some paint
But the marks soon grew faint
So now he just wears an old mac.

Paul Sidey

Welcome to the world of limericks – it's quite unlike any other!

You can see from the example above that you are in for a whole lot of fun.

A limerick is a very special kind of verse, but the beauty of it is that, although it is generally confined to five lines and has a very recognizable rhythm, within those five lines you can be as batty, daft, rude and as utterly nonsensical as you wish. It's a lovely way of being very clever and very silly at one and the same time.

The first really famous limerick writer was Edward Lear and he was so funny and absurd that his limericks were a runaway success with children of all ages, from 0–100. Several of his limericks are included here, so you can see for yourself. Since then the limerick hasn't looked back. Witty, outrageous, rib-tickling and topical, the limerick has something for everyone.

Limericks are found all over the place and there must be

limericks about every subject under the sun. Few can resist them – only with those people who have *absolutely* no sense of humour at all will they fail to raise a flicker of a smile. Most mums, dads, grandparents, aunts, uncles, sisters, brothers and friends like a good laugh, so bring this book out when someone is in need of cheering up, or even when you are in trouble . . . and see what happens.

Who knows? By the end of *A Dashing Young Tiger Named Jack* you may be so limerick-mad that you will want to have a go yourself. You could even organize a competition among your friends. Just to start you off, here is one you can practise on: see what you can write in the spaces provided.

There was once a young person of . . .
Who declared . . . . . .
A limerick or two,
When you're feeling blue,
. . . .

Have a wonderfully mad and silly time!

EXTREMELY SILLY

Just to get you in the mood, here is a selection of beautifully whacky limericks.

Great-grandfather at Waterloo
Fought solidly all the day through;
He slashed and he hacked,
Through bodies tight packed
And managed to reach platform two.
Frank Richards

Said the Boy King, 'I fear I've a funny
Feeling down here in my tummy.'
'Tut, tut!,' said old Ra,
'I can see that you are
Not a son, nor a dad, but a Mummy.'
John Letts

There was a young lady of Beccles
Whose face was infested with freckles:
But nobody saw
Not one facial flaw
For she had an abundance of shekels.
Anon

A foolish old farmer called Brow,
Gummed feathers all over a cow.
He said, 'Go and sing
You stupid great thing!
Don't you know you're a dicky-bird now?'
Edward O'Neil

A dentist named Archibald Moss
Fell in love with the dainty Miss Ross.
Since he held in abhorrence
Her Christian name, Florence,
He renamed her his dear dental floss.
Anon

There was an old loony of Lyme
Whose candour was simply divine.
When they asked, 'Are you there?'
He said, 'Yes, but take care,
For I'm never "all there" all the time.'
Anon

An earnest young lady called Botts
Could tie most incredible knots –
Double granny or reef
With a hitch underneath –
But none of them cleared up her spots.
Michael Palin

There was a young lady called Tony
With a nose incredibly bony;
Her hair was so long,
So thick, brown and strong
That she was taken for My Little Pony.
Elizabeth Buchan

There was a young man of Kilpeacon
Whose nose was as red as a beacon;
But by saying, 'It's white,'
Twenty times, day and night,
He cured it and died an Archdeacon.
Anon

There was a young man of Bengal
Who went to a fancy dress ball;
He went, just for fun,
Dressed up as a bun,
And a dog ate him up in the hall.
Anon

There was a baked bean in a tin
Who loved someone long, white and thin,
So he bought some confetti
And married the spaghetti
Before being thrown in the bin.
Emma Henderson

There was an old man of Tralee
Who was bothered to death by a flea,
So he put out the light,
Saying, 'Now he can't bite,
For he'll never be able to see.'
Anon

The thunder god felt rather chilly,
So he went for a ride on his filly.
'I'm Thor!,' he cried,
And the horse replied,
'You've forgotten your thaddle, you thilly.'
Janet Rogers

A modest young maid of New Hall
Met a man at a fancy dress ball;
He said, 'Isn't it rude
To be totally nude?' –
She replied, 'I'm Eve'ere the Fall.'
Anon

An alarm clock was given to Di,
From her mother, just back from Shanghai,
But her sister, Belinda,
Threw it out of the window,
'Cos she wanted to see the time fly.
Michelle Morris

There was a young cyclist from Theales
Who did curious things on his wheels;
He rode up in the air
With considerable flair
And did wheelies while clicking his heels.
Elizabeth Buchan

A lady I know from Norwich
Her accent is thick – thick as porridge.
She got it from poor folk
Who live down in Norfolk
And now calls a garage – 'a gorridge!'
Max Bygraves

On the chest of the barmaid at Sale
Were tattooed the prices of ale,
And on her behind
For the sake of the blind,
Was the same information in Braille.
Anon

There was a young man from New Delhi
Who kept all his cash in a welly,
But whoever he paid
Always said, 'I'm afraid
I can't take it. Your money's too smelly.'
Miles Kington

Is your schoolteacher such an old bag,
Does she pester and wheedle and nag?
And have you a hunch
When the bell goes for lunch
That she runs to the loo for a fag?
Michelle Morris

There was a young lady from Lop
Who drank a large bottle of pop;
She drank it so quick
Every sip, every lick
That she swallowed the bottle and top.
Julie Ling

Said a teacher with some indignation
To her class – 'You have ruined my Alsatian!
The ink blots you shied
Have adhered to his hide
And now he's a spotted Dalmatian!'
Leslie Crowther

A raja who hailed from Calcutta,
Would only consume bread and butter;
When served with hot curry,
He'd leave in a hurry,
And empty it into the gutter.
Barry Fantoni

A skeleton once in Khartoum
Invited a ghost to his room;
They spent the whole night
In the eeriest fight
As to who should be frightened of whom.
Anon

There was a fair flapper from Flodden
Whose foot by a stranger was trodden;
When he, to end strife,
Said 'Please be my wife.'
She retorted, 'But this is so sodden.'
Langford Reed

There was an old lady of Harrow
Who rode into church in a barrow;
When she stuck in the aisle
She exclaimed with a smile:
'They built these 'ere churches too narrow.'
Anon

There was an old lady of Weasenham,
Whose bed clothes had too many fleas in 'em.
So she covered her sheeting
With masses of Keating*
Which made all the fleas in 'em sneeze in 'em.
Richard Murdoch
* *a brand of flea powder*

SILLY ANIMALS

Some of the best and the funniest limericks are about animals . . .

There once was a rhino whose horn had turned pink,
They didn't know why; then they started to think,
'It's perfectly clear
It's the wine and the beer
Young Ronald the rhino had taken to drink!'
Valerie Hudson

A pheasant who feared to be shot
Told the hunter, 'A game bird I'm not!
I'm really a pullet,
So withhold your bullet.'
And the marksman was fooled by his plot.
Judy Allen

A certain old maid of Cohoes,
In despair, taught her bird to propose;
But the parrot dejected
At being accepted,
Spoke some words too profane to disclose.
Anon

There was an old lady of Worcester
Who was kept awake by a rooster,
So she cut off his head
And made sure he was dead
And now he can't crow like he used-ter.
Janet Rogers

Said a winkle, 'I wish I were thin.
This shell is so cramped when I'm in.
I'm getting so stout,
I'll never get out.
Can somebody lend me a pin?'
Frank Richards

There was once a brainy baboon
Who always breathed down a bassoon;
For he said, 'It appears
That in billions of years
I shall certainly hit on a tune.'
Sir Arthur Stanley Eddington

A talented young chimpanzee
Was keen to appear on TV.
He wrote to Brooke Bond
But they didn't respond
So he had to become an MP.
Wendy Cope

Our kitten, the one we call Louie,
Will never eat liver so chewy,
Nor the milk, nor the fish
That we put in his dish,
He only will dine on chop suey.
Anon

There was once a blooming Great Auk –
Couldn't fly – and hardly could walk.
The ignorant Picts
Used to beat it with sticks
For the pleasure of hearing it squawk.
John Letts

There was a young man from York,
Whose budgie began to squawk,
So he said with a grin,
As he pushed his beak in,
'I only like budgies that talk.'
Malcolm Farrow

Consider the lowering lynx,
He's savage and sullen and stynx,
Though he never has stunk
Like the scandalous skunk,
That's a task far beyond him methinks!
Langford Reed.

On the Number 3 bus t'other day
Two tigers were chatting away,
They'd been out to buy
Three shirts and a tie,
But no one had asked them to pay.

Paul Sidey

A cat in despondency sighed
And resolved to commit suicide.
She passed under the wheels
Of eight automobiles
And after the ninth one she died.

Anon

A young woman who'd come home to Blighty,
Said that elephants are really quite flighty,
'But if one's in your bed,
Then you'll know it,' she said,
' 'Cos an "E" will be sewn on its nightie.'

Michelle Morris

A dog from Sri Lanka called Patch
Sat down on a tree stump to scratch;
But he found that the flea,
Was not one, but three
And the first of a very large batch.

Michael Palin

Said a miserly peer at the Abbey,
'I fear I shall look rather shabby,
For I've replaced my ermine,
Infested with vermin,
With the fur of my dear defunct tabby.'
Anon

There once was a very young prawn,
Who didn't know how he'd been born,
And what was so rum
Was that nor did his mum
'Ask your dad,' she replied with a yawn.
Valerie Hudson

There was a young maiden called Maggie
Whose dog was hairy and shaggy;
The front end of him
Was vicious and grim
But the tail end was friendly and waggy.
Anon

I'm a wisp of a wasp with a worry,
I'm hiding somewhere in Surrey,
I've just bit upon
The fat sit-upon
Of the king – so I left in a hurry.
Colin West

'Tell me Tiger,' said Isobel Stranks,
'Have you always had stripes on your flanks?'
The Tiger said, 'No,
I'm ambitious and so
I just worked my way up from the ranks.'
Eric Sykes

We are very depressed with our Yak,
Which has now become terribly slak.
It cleaned kitchens and stairs
Better than many au pairs,
But now we're going to send our Yak bak.
Anon

There was once a centipede neat,
Who bought shoes for all of his feet;
'For,' he said, 'I might chance
To go for a dance,
And I must have my outfit complete.'
Anon

'I'm worried,' a kangaroo said,
'I'm sure that my baby's well fed,
But he tickles the tum
Of his loving old mum,
By eating his biscuits in bed.'
Frank Richards

There once was an old jelly fish,
Who said, very sadly, 'I wish
I lived in the Red Sea,
For then I would be
A redcurrant jelly fish.'
Anon

There was once a doughty young fly,
Who said, 'I will do it or die.'
So she took off her stocking,
A spectacle shocking,
And waded right into a pie.
Anon

There once was a corpulent carp,
Who wanted to play on the harp;
But to his chagrin
So short was his fin,
He couldn't reach up to C sharp.
Anon

There was a young lady of Guise
Who kept two performing fleas
Named Maurice and Mabel,
Which danced on the table,
And earned quite respectable fees.
Langford Reed

Some rabbits came over from Arden
And gobbled up most of my garden.
They feasted for hours
On stalks and on flowers
And never once said, 'Beg your pardon.'
Anon

While out on a walk one fine day
A horse that could talk blocked my way.
He might have been frightful,
Or even delightful –
But the poor thing had nothing to say.
Dyan Sheldon

SILLY FACTS

You might, or might not, find the following useful at school.

When you think of the hosts without number
Who are slain by the deadly cucumber,
It's such a mistake
Of such food to partake;
It results in permanent slumber.
Janet Rogers

Said a zealous young student named Coles,
'As we always term Poland folk "Poles",
I'm more than inclined,
With my logical mind,
To designate Holland's sons "Holes".'
Anon

The Romans had, so it appears,
IV limbs, I nose and II ears.
The toes of these men
All numbered to X
And they lived LX months in V years.
Frank Richards

A fellow from Bristol, called Neve,
Was seriously known to believe
That, the world being flat,
If once lost, your poor cat
Would be terribly hard to retrieve.
Michael Palin

There was a young fellow from Dice
Who remarked, 'Although bigamy's nice,
Even two are a bore;
I'd prefer three or four,
For the plural of spouse, it is spice.'
Anon

There once was a Plesiosaurus,
Who lived when the earth was all porous;
But it fainted with shame
When it first heard its name,
And departed long ages before us.
Anon

It's a very odd thing about vicars.
They rhyme with stickers and flickers
That's perfectly fine
Till you reach the last line
Which invariably ends up with 'knickers'.
Valerie Hudson

Said a rather dense schoolboy named Pete,
'Mathematics has fair got me beat.
I'm sure a square root
Is some sort of fruit,
And Pi is a nice thing to eat.'
Frank Richards

A cheese that was aged and grey
Was walking and talking one day,
Said the cheese, 'Kindly note
My mama was a goat
And I'm made out of curds, by the whey.'
Janet Rogers

If there's one thing Nature has taught us,
It's the virtues of being a tortoise.
They can slumber, I hear,
More than half of the year
In the depths of their snug winter-quartoise.

John Letts

Old Mother Hubbard went to the cupboard
To get her Alsatian some bread.
When she got there,
The cupboard was bare
So she ate the Alsatian instead!

Charlie Chester

SILLY HISTORY

From *1066 and All That* onwards, history has always been what you make of it.

Cleopatra observed, 'That false tale
Of the asp many ears may regale –
What a fuss they all make
About that poor snake!
Why, the poison was sent me by mail.'
Anon

There was a young lady from Pisa
Whose name was the Mona Lisa.
The cause of her smile
Is that she fell in a pile
Of tasty, hot anchovy pizza.
Jackie Shorey

Said Henry the Eighth, 'It's too bad.
I know it's six wives that I've had,
But I never knew
Who came after who.
It's enough to drive anyone mad.'
Frank Richards

In attempting to kill Rasputin
They tried poison, stabbing and shootin'.
When the man failed to die
They said, 'Just one more try,
Only this time try putting the boot in.'
Spike Milligan

There once was a diarist named Pepys,
Who wrote about London in hepys;
When the Fire died down
Pepys went about town
And culled tales that give one the crepys.
Hugh Powell

Said Wellington, 'What's the location
Of this battle I've won for the nation?'
They replied, 'Waterloo.'
He said, 'That'll do,
What a glorious name for a station.'
Frank Richards

There was a composer called Liszt,
Who from writing could never desiszt.
He made polonaises
Quite worthy of praises,
And now that he's gone, he is miszt.
Anon

There was an Egyptian from Cairo,
Who wrote hieroglyphs with a biro.
Tourists saw all his scrawls
On the pyramid walls
And thought they were drawn by the Pharoah.

Joan Brown

A soldier who fought at Culloden
Had to stop when his tootsies got trod on.
And when he got home,
He complained with a moan,
He was cold and his knickers were sodden.

David Hatch

There was once a Madame called Tussaud,
Who loved the grand folk in *Who's Who* so,
That she made them in wax,
Both their fronts and their backs,
And asked no permission to do so.
Charles Inge

There was a composer called Haydn
The field of sonata would waydn;
He wrote the *Creation*
Which made a sensation,
And this was the work which he daydn.
Anon

When Mary, Queen of Scots lost her head
The English announced she was dead.
They crammed in the bits
(It was a tight fit)
Into a coffin made entirely of lead.
Elinor Rose

There was a young man named Achilles
Whose wrongs always gave him the willies;
So he sulked in his tent
Like a half-witted gent,
Say, wasn't them heroes the sillies?
Edwin Meade Robinson

Said Moses to each Israelite,
'We've come to the Red Sea all right.
Now you can get started
When the waters have parted.
But wait for the little green light'.
Frank Richards

'This Sir Walter's becoming a joke',
Said Elizabeth choking on smoke.
'I was healthy before
He began to explore;
So I'll trample all over his cloak.'
Michelle Morris

When Shakespeare was aged and mellow,
He became a forgetful old fellow.
He was never quite clear
Whether he wrote 'MacLear',
Or 'The Two Merry Wives of Othello'.
Frank Richards

SILLY PEOPLE

What *did* happen to the fat lady from Skye, the old man in the tree, the merry old man of Oporto, a young lady called Rose, the young fellow from . . . ?

There was a young girl known as Sue
Who carried a frog in each shoe.
When asked to stop
She replied with a hop
'I'm trying to get in *Who's Zoo*.'

Janet Rogers

Said Bunter, 'It's easy to diet
For the rest of the term I shall try it.
The idea is this:
To give meals a miss
And eat lots of sweets on the quiet.'

Paul Rand

There was a young lady called Alice
Who wanted to live in the palace.
She went up to London
Was thrown in the dungeon,
Yet she still bears the Windsors no malice.

Andrew Jones

An American lady called Hannah
Once slipped on a peel of 'banana'.
As she lay on her side,
More stars she espied
Than there are in the Star-spangled Banner.
Janet Rogers

An old archaeologist, Throstle,
Discovered a marvellous fossil.
He knew from its bend
And the nail on the end
'Twas the finger of Paul the Apostle.
Anon

A young man from down in Laguna
Once fell in love with a tuna.
The affair, although comic,
Was so economic
He wished he had thought of it suna.

Anon

An astronaut, one afternoon,
Signalled, 'I'm coming down soon.
I've had such a fright
From a very strange sight –
A cow jumping over the moon.'

Frank Richards

A lady from near Lake Louise
Declared she was bothered by fleas.
She used gasoline
And later was seen
Sailing over the hills and the trees.

Anon

A professor named Aubrey Brett
Said, 'Three things I always forget.
That's all my friends' names,
And the times of the trains
And the third one I can't recall yet!'

Janet Rogers

There was an old woman of Filey,
Who valued old candle-ends highly;
When no one was looking
She used them for cooking.
'It's wicked to waste,' she said drily.
Anon

There was a fat lady from Skye
Who was sure she was going to die.
But for fear that once dead
She would not be well-fed
She gulped down a pig, a cow, a sheep,
twelve buns, a seven-layer cake,
four cups of coffee and a green apple pie!
Anon (*Phew! – Ed.*)

A huntsman pursuing a pheasant
Shot a farmer, three pigs and a peasant,
A milkmaid, a cow,
And a rather fat sow;
Then he said, 'That's enough for the present.'
Janet Rogers

There was a young lady of Stroud
Whose voice was so awfully loud;
When she went for a walk,
They forbade her to talk,
For fear of attracting a crowd.
Anon

There was an old man of the Cape
Who made himself garments of crêpe.
When they asked, 'Do they tear?'
He replied, 'Here and there,
But they're perfectly splendid for shape.'
Robert Louis Stevenson

There was once a student named Bessor
Whose knowledge grew lessor and lessor.
It at last grew so small
He knew nothing at all
And today he's a college professor.
Anon

There was a young lady of Poole
Who thought she would set up a school;
But all she could teach
Was nine parts of speech
And how to make gooseberry fool.
Anon

There was a young lady from Dereham
The boys wouldn't let her go near 'em.
She said, 'Have I BO?'
They said, 'Dear me no!
It's your fags, luv, you know we can't bear 'em.'
Margaret Clarke

I said to a man of Norwich,
Who sat by the side of a ditch,
'On an anthill you sit,
I'd have thought you'd be bit!'
He answered, 'I am – and I itch.'
Anon

A bad-tempered man named McDade
Ate breakfast with rake, hoe and spade.
While wearing his slippers
He liked to eat kippers
And sausages with sweet marmalade.
Marguerite Varday

There was a young person of Ayr
Whose head was remarkably square;
On top in fine weather
She wore a gold feather,
Which dazzled the people of Ayr.
Edward Lear

There was a young fellow named Tuttle
Whose ways were exceedingly subtle.
He thought it a bore
To go in the front door,
So he entered by way of the scuttle.
Anon

My sister's remarkably light,
She can float to a fabulous height.
It's a tiresome thing,
But we tie her with string,
And use her instead of a kite.
Margaret Mahy

There dwelt an old woman at Exeter
When visitors came it sore vexed her;
So for fear they should eat
She locked up all the meat,
This stingy old woman of Exeter.
Anon

A colonel who used to assert
That naught his digestion could hurt,
Was forced to admit
That his weak point was hit
When they gave him hot shot for dessert.
Anon

A body painter with colours obsessed
Found that Burnt Umber made him depressed.
So he turned to shades gladder,
Green – Orange – Rose Madder,
And daubed traffic lights on his chest.
Judy Allen

There was a young fellow called Doyle,
Who wrapped his wife up in tin foil;
For he said, 'She's so sweet,
And she is such a treat
I'm terribly afraid she will spoil.'
Anon

There was a young lady named Rose
Who had a huge wart on her nose;
When she had it removed
Her appearance improved,
But her glasses slipped down to her toes.
Janet Rogers

There was an old maid of Oneida,
Who screamed at the sight of a spider,
She would faint at a ram,
And flee from a lamb
But fearlessly tackle a tiger.
Anon

There was a young lady whose eyes
Were unique as to colour and size;
When she opened them wide,
People turned aside,
And started away in surprise.
Edward Lear

A muddled young lady called Rita
Buys her paper and flour by the metre.
She gets ribbon and jam
Weighed out by the gramme
And orders her cheese by the litre.
Anon

A sad young cadet from Provence
Who sliced off his legs with a lance,
Got hold of some glue,
Stuck them back, good as new,
And swaggered off out to a dance.
A. & D. Newlands

A gentleman living at Harwich,
At ninety was thinking of marriage;
In came his grandson,
Who was just twenty-one,
And went off with the bride in the carriage.
Anon

There was a young girl from Prestatyn
Who made herself knickers of satin.
For her classical friends
To peruse as she bends,
She embroidered the edges in Latin.
David Hatch

A young boy who once, for a bet
Tried to copy the family pet;
He quite lost his temper
When the dog got distemper
And they *both* had to go to the vet.
Valerie Hudson

There was an old fellow of Trinity,
A doctor well versed in Divinity;
But he took to free thinking
And then to deep drinking,
And so had to leave the vicinity.
Anon

There was an old man in a tree,
Whose whiskers were lovely to see;
But the birds of the air
Pluck'd them perfectly bare,
To make themselves nest in that tree.

Edward Lear

In Japan a fat tourist from Surrey
Ate his curry in too great a hurry;
He stuffed like a goat
Till it stuck to his throat,
And the coroner said, 'Hurri-curri.'*

Anon

* *Hara-kiri is a Japanese way of committing suicide.*

There was a young lady of Pandy
Who drank a large tumbler of brandy;
In a moment her eyes
Turned to gooseberry pies
And her hair, that was black, became sandy.
Anon

There was an old German at Cowes,
Who appeared in an elegant blouse;
When they cried, 'You look dire
In your female attire.'
He replied, 'It ain't mine, it's the Frau's.'
Langford Reed

A merry old man of Oporto
Had long had the gout in his fore toe,
And oft when he spoke
To relate a good joke
A terrible twinge cut him short O!
Anon

There was a young lady of Kent
Who always said just what she meant;
People said, 'She's a dear –
So unique – so sincere – '
But they shunned her by common consent.
Janet Rogers

THE SMILE ON THE FACE OF THE TIGER . . .

Guess who has the last laugh?

There was an old man who was bitten
By forty-two cats and a kitten;
Cried he, 'It is clear
My end is quite near:
No matter, I'll die like a Briton.'
Anon

There was a young lady of Riga,
Who went for a ride on a tiger;
They returned from the ride
With the lady inside
And the smile on the face of the tiger.
Cosmo Monkhouse

There once was a very old gnu,
Who was used by a chief in some stew.
He should have been told
The gnu was too old:
For stews, only new gnus will do.
Anon

There was a sea-serpent of Salamanca
Which bit into a warship and sank 'er.
He ate all the crew –
A cruel thing to do –
And then picked his teeth with the anchor.
Anon

There was a young lady of Clare,
Who was sadly pursued by a bear;
When she found she was tired,
She abruptly expired,
That unfortunate Lady of Clare.
Edward Lear

There was once a man who said, 'Why
Can't I look that big snake in the eye?'
The snake said, 'But you can.'
And he looked at the man
(Most any last line will apply.)
Anon

There was a young girl called Ann
Who fried her goldfish in a pan,
Adding salt and then pepper
Didn't make it taste better –
And then she was sick over Gran.
Simon Cann

There once was a lady called Tate
Who won a live bear at a fête,
To her home it was led,
But it hadn't been fed,
And the police got there seconds too late.
Michael Palin

There was a young lady of Malta
Who strangled her aunt with a halter.
She said, 'I won't bury her,
She'll do for my terrier;
She'll keep for a month if I salt her.'
Anon

You will find by the banks of the Nile,
The haunts of the great crocodile.
He will welcome you in
With an innocent grin –
Which gives way to a satisfied smile.
John Letts

I live with a humorous cat
Who begs to be stroked and then SPLAT!
She gnashes her jaws,
Inserts all her claws
And laughs while you bleed on the mat.
Judy Allen

The sultan got sore of his harem
And invented a scheme for to scare 'em;
He caught him a mouse
Which he loosed in the house
(The confusion is called harem-scarem).
Janet Rogers

There was a young lady of Ryde,
Who was carried too far by the tide;
A man-eating shark
Said, 'How's this for a lark?
I knew that the Lord would provide.'
Anon

There was a young man of Belfast,
Who ran in a race and came last.
He said 'That's enough!
I'm all out of puff!'
As a tortoise came thundering past.

Anon

There was a cute fellow named Noah
Who knew when rain came it would pour.
So he built a nice ark
But thought it no lark
When the elephant stuck in the door.

N. Saunders

There once was an old Anaconda,
Who sat down to read *Daniel Deronda*
Which he calmly explained
Was all that remained
Of a book agent from Tonawanda.
Anon

A chap who loved fox-hunting madly,
Said, 'I'd give it up perfectly gladly
Were it not for the fear
(Here he shed a quiet tear)
That the foxes would miss it too badly.'
T. L. McCarthy

There was a young girl named O'Brien
Who taught holy hymns to a lion.
Of the lady there's some
In the lion's tum-tum;
The rest twangs a harp up in Sion.
Anon

R.I.P.

Be warned! There are some untimely ends in this section.

There was a young lad of St Just
Who ate apple pie till he bust;
It wasn't the fru-it
That caused him to do it,
What finished him off was the crust.
Anon

The day the vicar got drowned
Just a floating dog collar was found;
He's a watery vicar
With a one-legged knicker
And frilly attachments all round!
Kenny Everett

There was an old person of Tartary,
Who divided his jugular artery;
But he screeched to his wife,
And she said, 'Oh my life!
Your death will felt by all Tartary!'
Edward Lear

A novice was driving a car,
When down Porlock his son said, 'Papa,
If you drive at this rate
We are bound to be *late* –
Drive faster!' – He did, and they are!
Anon

There once was a phantom named Pete
Who never would play, drink or eat.
He said, 'I don't care
For a coke or eclair,
Can't you see that I'm dead on my feet?'
Janet Rogers

There was an old man called Rus,
Who was knocked down by a bus,
When asked, 'Are you dead?'
He nodded his head,
And caused quite a bit of a fuss.
Pamela Murphy

There was an old man and his wife,
Who lived in the bitterest strife;
He opened the stove,
Pushed her in with a shove,
And cried, 'There, you pest of my life.'
Anon

Ebenezer and Florence from Bow
Went out in a small boat to row,
But before very long . . .
Well, the tide was too strong!
Now their friends call the pair Ebb and Flo.

T. L. McCarthy

There was an old fellow of Lympne, *
Who said, 'How I wish I was slim!'
So he lived for three weeks
On nuts and two leeks,
And that was the last heard of him.

Anon

* *pronounced Limb*

'Will you beam me up, Scotty? There's two
Space invaders preparing a stew.
They have tied me up tightly,
And salted me lightly . . .
Hey Scotty! Am I getting through?'

T.L. McCarthy

There was an old fellow of Tonga,
Who was frightened to death by a conger;
And a medico said,
When he found he was dead,
'What a pity his nerves were not stronger!'

Anon

There was a young person named Ned
Who dined before going to bed
On lobster and jam
Some salad and ham,
And when he awoke, he was dead.

Janet Rogers

There was a young girl of Uttoxeter,
Whose brothers, one day, on a rock set her
While they went for a sail,
But were wrecked in a gale,
So the penguins and seagulls in flocks ate her.

Anon

I had a young pupil called Ned,
Who was fearfully thick in the head.
He could count up to five
And appeared to survive,
But by twenty to six he was dead.
Anon

There was a young man from the City.
The way that he drove was a pity;
The 30-mile sign
Was a pretty design.
His widow gets all of the kitty.
C. Carter

I will tell you a sad little tale
Of a rambler from Chapel-le-Dale:
On Ingelborough Hill
He fell down Gaping Gill;
They're returning the pieces by mail.
David Hatch

A certain young man of great gumption,
Among cannibals had the presumption
To go – but, alack!
He never came back,
They say he died of consumption.
Anon

There once was a horrible smell
The worst you ever heard tell.
They died in droves
And were laid out in rows
Plus the office cat as well.
Adam Peters

There was a young fellow called Hyde
Who fell down the privy and died;
His unfortunate brother
Fell into another
And now they're interred side by side.
Anon

There was a young lady of Ryde,
Who ate some green apples and died.
The apples fermented
Inside the lamented
And made cider inside her inside.
Anon

BLOOD 'N' GUTS

This section is devoted to all that is horrible, smelly, disgusting, sticky and creepy.

There was a young girl of the Somme,
Who sat on a number five bomb,
She thought it a dud 'un,
But it went off sudden –
Her exit she made with aplomb.
Anon

A sausage-maker who drove with great dash
Was involved in a motorway crash,
His car, I am told,
Was terribly old,
And he's now known as banger and smash.
Barry Fantoni

A nasty old vampire named Dracula,
Had habits really spectacular;
He drank by the keg,
But 'twas pure rhesus neg
– Red Barrel, to use the vernancular.
A. P. Cox

There was a young fellow of Herts,
Who, wishing to get into Barts
When next up in town,
On the tramlines lay down:
He was taken to Barts in three carts!
Anon

A surgeon from Glasgow named Mac,
Once forgot to put everything back.
As his train made to start,
His case came apart,
And a kidney rolled down off the rack.
Michael Palin

There once was a fellow called Topping
Who fell down five flights without stopping.
The janitor swore
As the clunk hit the floor,
'It will take the whole afternoon mopping.'
Anon

A girl from a nice convent school
Was wicked, sadistic and cruel.
One night, just for fun,
She set fire to a nun,
Screaming, 'Oh, what a silly old fuel.'
Spike Milligan

A youthful beef-packer named Young,
One day, when his nerves were unstrung,
Pushed his wife's ma – unseen –
In the chopping machine,
Then canned and labelled her 'Tongue'.
Anon

The Hoover in grim silence sat
But sucking no more at the mat;
Quietly it grunted
And slowly it shunted,
And messily disgorged the cat.
David Woodsford

There was a young monk of Siberia,
Who of fasting grew wearier and wearier,
Till, at length, with a yell,
He broke from his cell,
And devoured the Father Superior.
Anon

Said a puzzled young gardener named Sue,
Who had just cut a poor worm in two,
'Oh, I know I'm to blame
But both ends look the same!
So which do I say "Sorry" to?'
E. O. Parrott

There was an old fellow of Spain,
Whose leg was cut off by a train.
When his friends said, 'How sad.'
He replied, 'I am glad,
For I've now lost my varicose vein.'
Anon

A gourmet, deceased, from Prescali
Required a PM on his belly.
Pathology said
That the fellow was dead
From an excess of lamb and mint jelly.
David Hatch

Said a foolish young housewife of Wales:
'A smell of escaped gas prevails.'
So she searched with a light,
And, later that night,
Was collected in several pails.
Langford Reed

There was a young lady of Spain
Who was dreadfully sick in the train,
Not once, but again
And again, and again
And again, and again, AND AGAIN.
Anon

A wicked old butcher called Slye
Told the most terrible lie.
He developed a cough,
His fingers dropped off,
And he ended up stuffed in a pie.
Barry Fantoni

A cannibal bold of Penzance
Ate an uncle and two of his aunts,
A cow and her calf,
An ox and a half –
And now he can't button his pants.
Anon

The shortage of fuel made it hard
To maintain the big blaze in our yard;
We threw on Aunt Flo,
Who heightened the glow,
But I fear she became somewhat charred.
Langford Reed

At a bull fight in sunny Madrid
A tourist went clean off his lid.
He made straight for the bull,
While the crowd yelled, 'The fool
Will go home on a slab!' – and he did.
Anon

The spirit of Salisbury Plain
Wandered all night in the rain;
When the people said 'Oh.'
He replied, 'Yes, I know,
But something is dead in the drain.'
Anon

There was an old girl of Hong Kong
Whose breath was uncommonly strong,
Said she, 'I find onions
Are good for my bunions,
So I nibble 'em all the day long.'
Anon

There was an old lady of Hake,
Who said, 'I will bake a fine cake.'
She threw in some stones
And a bag of old bones,
Three trowels, two forks and a rake.

F. O. Brewster

There was a young man of Cornell,
Who said, 'I'm aware of a smell,
But whether its drains
Or human remains
I'm really unable to tell.'

Anon

There was a young girl called O'Neill
Who went up in the great Ferris wheel;
But when half-way round
She looked at the ground
And it cost her a 100p meal!

Anon

A headmaster's son called McNaught
Got a fright of the nastiest sort.
For when cleaning his teeth
He found bits of Keith
And others his father once taught.

Michael Palin

There was a young lady of Stornaway
Who by walking had both her feet worn away.
Said she, 'I won't mind
If only I find
That it's taken that terrible corn away.'

Anon

There was a young girl from Malacca
Who gave up the use of tobacca,
Saying, 'X-rays have shown
That my left lung had gone,
While the right one got blacka and blacka.'

T. L. McCarthy

There once was a girl called Rose,
Did very odd things with her toes,
(A naughty young miss
You mustn't do this)
She used them for picking her nose.
Valerie Hudson

There was a disgusting old man
Who used to eat catch-as-catch-can.
He covered his vest
With the remains of the best
Of the gravy, chicken and ham.
Anon

OH BAD LUCK!

It could happen to anyone . . .

There was a young druggist named Abel,
Who forgot to stick on the label.
It was poison within,
But was taken for gin;
He died at the end of a cable.
Anon

There was a young pilot from Bangor,
Who took a small plane from its hangar.
He flew it quite well
Till he hit the church bell,
When he dropped what you might call a clanger.
David Hatch

There was a young hiker called Hilda
Who went for a hike on St Kilda.
They say that the climb
Is really sublime:
But it wasn't for Hilda – it killed her.
John Letts

There was an old lady whose folly
Induced her to sit in the holly!
Whereupon, by a thorn
Her dress being torn
She quickly became melancholy.
Edward Lear

A horrible boy, name of Bobby
Collected fat worms as a hobby
He took some to sell
To a swanky hotel
And dropped the whole lot in the lobby.
Janet Allen

There was an old man who averred
He had learnt to fly like a bird.
Cheered by thousands of people
He leapt from the steeple –
His tomb states the date it occurred.
Anon

There was a young lady from Blaenau,
Who went for a ride on a rhino.
When it dropped dead,
She ungraciously said:
'We could use this poor rhino for lino.'
David Hatch

A near-sighted fellow named Walter
Led a glamorized lass to the altar,
A beauty he thought her
Till some soap and hot water
Made her look like the rock of Gibraltar.
Anon

A serving maid known as Maria,
Had problems in lighting the fire.
The wood being green,
She used gasoline . . .
And now her position's much higher.
Janet Rogers

There was a young lady of Trim,
Who attempted the channel to swim,
But a ravenous porpoise
Intercepted her corpus:
We will now sing the fifty-fifth hymn.
Langford Reed

When she took that walk down the aisle
She was dressed in the latest of staisle.
But a friend later said,
With the shake of her haid,
That her petticoat hung down a maisle.
Anon

Said the dentist to Sarah, 'How thrilling,
I must give you a dirty great filling.
Sarah's jaw opened wide,
Till the man fell inside
So he never did finish his drilling!
Michelle Morris

There was a fair maid of Ostend
Who thought she'd hold out to the end.
But half-way over
'Twixt Calais and Dover
She was sick – which she didn't intend.
Anon

This morning we have to deplore
The Bishop of Wigan's no more.
Last night at the Mayor's
He fell down the stairs:
The funeral's on Friday, at four.

Langford Reed

An opera star named Maria
Always tried to sing higher and higher,
Till she hit the high note
Which got stuck in her throat –
Then she entered the heavenly choir.

Anon

There was a young soldier called Edser.
When wanted was always in bed sir;
One morning at one,
They fired the gun
And Edser, in bed sir, was dead Sir!

Spike Milligan

There was a young woman from Thrace,
Whose nose spread all over her face.
She had very few kisses;
The reason for this is
There wasn't a suitable place.

Anon

There was a young lady of Cheadle,
Who was deeply beloved by the beadle;
But she scoffed at his prayer,
Left her work on his chair,
And the beadle sat down on the needle.

Anon

A girl named 'Ardwick was struck
With a cricket ball – 'out for a duck'
Her tombstone's lonely
With these words only –
' 'Ardwick – 'ard ball – 'ard luck'.

Charlie Chester

A facetious young bowler from Stoke
Bowled a hand grenade once for a joke.
But he ran out of luck
When the firing pin stuck,
Leaving only black flannels and smoke.

Ian Botham

There was a young lady named Stella
Fell in love with a bow-legged fella,
The venturesome chap,
Let her sit in his lap
And she fell clean through to the cella.

Anon

Said a general over at Tooting,
'We've some splendid young marksmen recruiting:
But their training, you see,
Isn't all it should be,
For there's no one in Tooting worth shooting.'
T. L. McCarthy

In Iceland, a supple young miss
Enthused, 'I think skating is bliss.'
This no more will she state
For a slip of the skate
Left her ending up something like this.
Anon

An optimist living at Datchet
Attempted to shave with a hatchet.
When his nose he did sever,
He said, 'Now I'll never
Have nasal catarrh – I can't catch it.'
Langford Reed

A vain little lady of Pisa,
Who thought she was like Mona Lisa,
Expected each day
To be stolen away –
But nobody wanted to seize her.
Anon

There was a young lady of Dorset,
Had a match and decided to toss it
In a can of benzine;
Then out on the green,
They found a side comb and a corset.

Anon

A trainee magician named Mick
Made a frightful mistake with a trick,
When he turned a small boy,
His mum's pride and joy,
Irreversibly into a brick.

Michael Palin

A high-minded teacher from Nosh
Who sought to make all pupils posh,
When made a new head
Of a London co-ed
Was bashed on the conk with a cosh.
David Hatch

There was a young chap from Trieste,
Who in summer would wear a string vest,
He was known far and near
For his odd choice of gear,
But he never got called the best dressed!
Michelle Morris

Said a pretty young girl, 'I shall smother
That nasty young twerp of a brother.
I've just heard him say
I'll be fifty next May,
And he's told all the boys I'm his mother!'
Frank Richards

There was a young lad from Northwold
Who was most incredibly bold.
When he climbed up a pylon,
He still had his smile on,
It goes well with a halo of gold.
R. Crisp

VERY RUDE

This section is not for grown-up consumption

There was a young fellow from Fife,
Who didn't know one fact of life.
He only got naughty
When he married – at forty
And found them all out from his wife.
Valerie Hudson

A cute debutante from Saint Paul
Wore a newspaper dress to a ball;
The dress caught on fire
And burnt her entire
Front page, sporting section and all.
Anon

To an artist a husband named Bicket
Said, 'Turn your backside and I'll kick it.
You have painted my wife
In the nude to the life:
Do you think for one moment that's cricket?'
John Galsworthy

A plumber who lived in East Dene,
Designed an unusual latrine,
When seated you found
It emitted no sound:
When you rose it played, 'God Save the Queen'.
A & D Newlands

There was a young lady called Nellie,
Who constructed rude scenes on her belly.
The carving was great,
The plaster ornate,
But the detail's what got her on telly.
Andrew Jones

An athletic young lady of Clewer
Once incited a bull to pursue her;
But she vaulted the gate
Just a fraction too late,
Now when she sits down she says, 'Oo-er.'
Anon

There was a young lad called Billy
Who constantly flashed his . . . . .
The folks all round
Kept their eyes on the ground
And whispered: 'Won't he, or will he?'
Elizabeth Buchan

There was a young lady from Whitton
Whose hot pants (or so it was written),
Were too small for her bottom,
And as they were cotton
They split, and her bottom was bitten.
E. R. Franklin

There was a young maid from Madras,
Who had the most beautiful ass.
Not, what you think,
Round, dimpled and pink;
It was grey, had long ears and ate grass.
Anon

I sat next to the Duchess at tea,
It was just as I feared it would be:
Her rumblings abdominal
Were truly phenomenal,
And everyone thought it was me!
Woodrow Wilson

There was once a Dominican friar
Who was seized with unholy desire:
And the primary cause
Was the Abbess's drawers,
Which were airing in front of the fire.
Anon

EVEN *MORE* RUDE

Nor is this one . . .

There was a most finicky lass
Who wore panties constructed of brass.
When they asked, 'Don't they chafe?'
She said, 'Yes, but I'm safe
Against pinchers and snakes in the grass.'
Anon

The vicar of Pevensey Bay
Went abroad for a year and a day.
His flock, off the tether,
Assembled together,
And took a decision to stray.
A. & D. Newlands

There was a lady of Erskine,
Who had a remarkably fair skin.
When I said to her, 'Mabel,'
You look well in your sable.'
She replied, 'I look best in my bearskin.'
Anon

A buxom young lady of Bude
Remarked, 'Men are exceedingly rude;
When I bathe in the sea
They all follow me
To see if my bosoms protrude.'
Anon

There was a young lady called Burton,
Who outraged the Fellows of Girton,
By cycling to town
Without wearing a gown
And, what's worse, without even a skirton.
John Letts

There was a young woman of Aenos,
Who came to our party as Venus.
We told her how rude
'Twas to come there quite nude
And we brought her a leaf from the greenh'us.
Anon

An extremely odd vicar from Bude,
Decided to preach in the nude.
When his bishop got wind,
He said, son, you have sinned,
And behaved most incredibly rude.
Barry Fantoni

There once was a monk in Siberia,
Whose existence grew steadily drearier,
Till he broke from his cell
With a hell of a yell
And eloped with the Mother Superior.
Anon

An explorer named Mortimer Craft,
While in Africa ate spiced giraffe.
The effect of this food
Was a sound deep and rude
And green flames that shot out fore and aft.
David Hatch

There was a young lady of Wilts
Who walked all through Scotland on stilts;
When they said, 'Oh how shocking
To show so much stocking!'
She said, 'How about you and your kilts?'
Anon

There was a young lady named Bianca,
Who retired while the ship lay at anchor;
But awoke in dismay
When she heard the mate say,
We must pull off the top sheet and spanker.'
Anon

SILLY BILLIES

Here are some more limericks which are about people who are . . . well . . . *very* silly.

There was a small maiden named Anne,
Who thought she could walk to Japan,
But was weary and spent
Before she reached Kent
And had to come home in a van.

Langford Reed

There was a young man from Darjeeling
Who got on a bus bound for Ealing.
It said on the door:
'Please don't spit on the floor'.
So he got up and spat on the ceiling.

Anon

Billy Fitzwilliam McBold
Believed everything he was told.
He came late to the kitchen
Wearing jumper and mittens
Because he'd heard that his tea had gone cold.

Dyan Sheldon

There was a young lady called Viccars,
Who had no control over her knickers.
They would twist round her knee
During afternoon tea
And the result was plenty of snikkers.
Elizabeth Buchan

There was a young lady of Tottenham,
Who's no manners or else she's forgotten 'em.
At tea at the vicar's,
She tore off her knickers,
Because, she explained, she felt 'ot in 'em.
Anon

There once was a schoolboy from Dover
Who trained a pet sheepdog called Rover.
They both ran for miles
And jumped over stiles
Till they dropped, tired out, in the clover.
Ruth Spencer

There was a young woman of Ayr,
Tried to steal out of church during prayer;
But the squeak of her shoes
So enlivened the pews
That she sat down again in despair.
Anon

There was a young lady named Rood
Who was such a queer little prude,
She pulled down the blind
When changing her mind
Lest some passer-by should intrude.

Anon

A footballer with a sore toe
Reported to the physio.
When the team saw his strapping
They all began clapping
'Cos he'd finished it off with a bow.

Don Howe

There was a young lady of Natchez
Who sat in some nettle-wood patches.
Now she lies on her face
With an awful grimace
And scratches and scratches and scratches.
Anon

A man known as Finicky Fred
Found some spiders alive in his bread.
He let out a shout
Saying, 'Nowt's taken out,
But I'd rather the spiders were dead.'
Janet Allen

There was a young maid who said, 'Why
Can't I look in my ear with my eye?
If I give my mind to it,
I'm sure I can do it,
You never can tell till you try.'
Anon

At a café, a man next to me
Ordered twenty-two candles for tea.
When I murmured 'How quaint.'
He replied 'No, it ain't
I'm on a light diet, you see.'
Frank Richards

A prudish old lady called Muir
Had a mind so incredibly pure,
That she fainted away
At a friend's house one day
At the sight of a canary's manure.
Anon

The vicar who lived in Berlin,
Came to mamma to talk about sin.
When she offered him tea,
He refused politely
And requested a pint of pink gin.
Michelle Morris

There was a Portuguese from Algarve,
Who determined not to starve.
He found the biggest sardine,
That you ever have seen,
From which each day of the week he would carve.
Joan Brown

We have a good cook called Clarissa,
And someone attempted to kiss her,
So now she won't stay,
Unless every day,
That happens again to Clarissa.
Anon

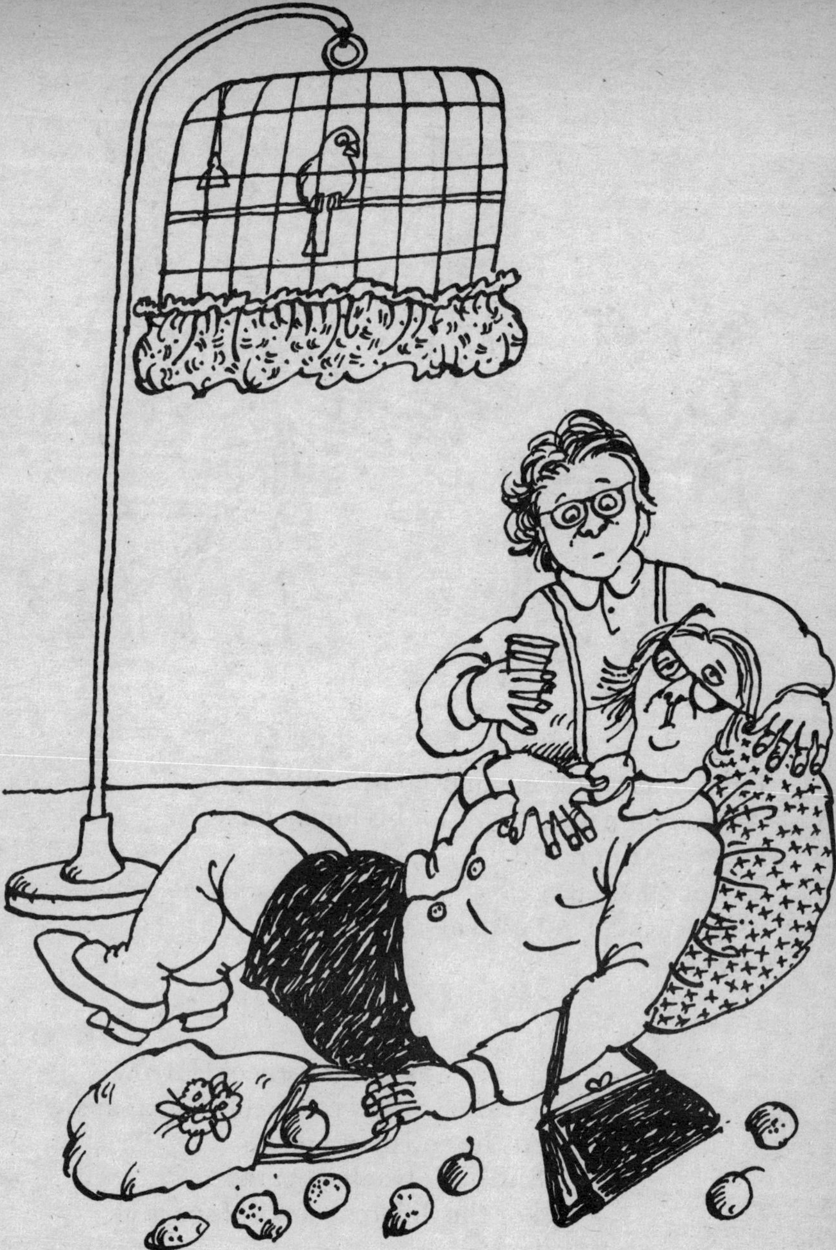

There was a policeman from Munchen
Who seldom went home for his luncheon,
From a farmer he'd beg,
The occasional egg,
And beat it all up with his truncheon.
Barry Fantoni

There was an old lady of Harrow
Whose views were exceedingly narrow.
At the end of her paths
She built two bird baths
For the different sexes of sparrow.
Anon

There was a young lady of Cheadle;
Who sat down in church on a needle,
Though deeply imbedded
'Twas luckily threaded,
So she had it removed by the beadle.
Anon

My friend who lives in Madrid
Really shouldn't have done what she did.
She ran into the Prado
With a ripe avocado
And ate lunch by a sketch of El Cid!
Michelle Morris

A timorous maiden named Anne,
With an abnormal hatred of man,
Is transfixed with fear
When she sees one draw near,
And skedaddles as fast as she can.
Anon

Eleanora Rosemary Toucan
Was as mild and as meek as a lamb
'Till she ran off to France
And proceeded to dance
The wildest ever can-can.
Elinor Rose

There's a girl out in Ann Arbor, Mich.,
To meet with I never would wich,
She'd gobble ice-cream
Till with colic she'd scream,
Then order another big dich.

Anon

A ventriloquist taking a nap,
Let his dummy fall out of his lap.
He said, while still dozing,
'I'll punch your fat nose in.'
And woke himself up with a slap.

Barry Fantoni

A safe-cracking thief called MacBride
Once blew a safe-door open wide,
When the dust cleared away
He was filled with dismay,
For he found there was nothing inside.

Janet Rogers

IF TWO OR MORE MOUSES ARE MICE – OR SILLY PRONUNCIATIONS

The English language is full of strange spellings and funny rules. This section is all about having fun with words – just mucking about for the sheer pleasure of it – and the result is often hilarious.

A poor fellow living at Costessey,
Had a wife who was terribly bostessey.
'If you are late home,' she said
With a toss of her head,
'I shall know you've been flirting with Flostessie.'

Ida Thurtle

If two or more mouses are mice,
And a handful of louses are lice,
I understand why –
As the rule must apply –
A handful of rouses are rice.

Anon

There was an old girl of Uganda,
Renowned for her coolness and candour,
When during abuse,
Her spouse yelled, 'You goose!'
She quickly retorted, 'Uganda!'
Langford Reed

I know an old man of Durazzo,
I've never known anyone chazzo;
From the moment he's begun
Till the moment he's done
I can only say, 'Really is thazzo?'
Anon

Jane pinched her sister Miranda
While sitting out on the veranda.
Miranda said 'Cow!
I will push you off now!'
But her mother screamed, 'Randa, unhand her!'
Dyan Sheldon

A brother when asked by the Prior
Why he spent so much time by the fire,
Said, 'While all of you pray,
I sit here all day –
In fact, I'm your chip-monk, or friar.'
Anon

There was a professor of Caius*
Who measured six foot round the knaius;
He went down to Harwich
Nineteen in the carriage
And found it a terrible squaius.

Conrad Aitken

* *pronounced Keys*

A lady, an expert on skis,
Went out with a man who said, 'Plis
On the next precipice
Will you give me a kiss?'
She said, 'Quick! Before somebody sis.'

Anon

Young William was up to skullduggery
(He thought he was a bit of a thuggery).
But one day he got sloshed
By a policeman's cosh
And punched all over his muggery.
Adam Peters

There was an old fellow of Norwich
Who was awfully fond of cold porwich.
As it was never served
He quietly observed;
'I'll go into the pantry and forwich.'
Anon

An irresolute gardener from Bute
Who at first thought chrysanthemums cute,
Got hooked on a hedge
And then finally veg
And declared that you could not beet root.
Gordon Newlands

In my road there's a hole, or declavity,
Which attracts men of invasive procalivity.
One group of them drills it
A different one fills it
In regular, alternate, activity.
Judy Allen

The bottle of perfume that Willie sent
Was highly displeasing to Millicent.
Her thanks were so cold,
They quarrelled, I'm told,
Through the silly scent Willie sent Millicent.
Anon

A flea and a fly in a flue
Were imprisoned so what could they do?
Said the fly, 'Let us flee.'
Said the flea, 'Let us fly.'
So they flew through a flaw in the flue.
Anon

There was a young maid in Tahiti
Whom the neighbours considered quite flahiti,
For if Monday was fine
She would hang on the line
An extremely diaphanous nahiti.
Anon

An obstinate lady of Leicester
Wouldn't marry her swain, though he preicester.
For his income, I fear,
Was a hundred a year
On which he could never have dreicester.
Anon

A sleeper from the Amazon
Put nighties of his gra'mazon.
The reason, that
He was too fat
To get his own pajamazon.
Anon

There was a young woman of Welwyn
Loved a barman, who served at the 'Belwyn'.
But the 'Belwyn', oh dear!
Had a well in the rear
So they never got wed, for they felwyn.
Anon

A young man of imposing physique
Bathed every night in a chrique!
Till one day it ran dry
When he said, with a sigh
'Why the thing must have sprung a bad lique!'
Anon

There was a young lady from Leeds
Who wanted some cash for her needs.
She proposed to a baker
Who did not forsake her –
Now she's got all the dough that she kneads.
Bob Monkhouse

Said a constable stern on his beat,
To a couple more fond than discreet,
'Though a Miss miss a kiss,
Give the next kiss a "miss",
For a kiss is amiss in the street.'
Anon

A traveller once to his sorrow
Requested a ticket to Morrow.
Said the agent, 'It's plain
That there isn't a train
To Morrow today, but tomorrow!'
Janet Rogers

A beautiful lady named Psyche
Is loved by a fellow named Yche.
One thing about Ych
The lady can't lych
Is his beard, which is dreadfully pspyche.
Anon

'I've toothache,' moaned my brother, Don.
'Don't worry,' said dear Uncle John.
'Just crash your head
Through the window instead,
And you'll find that the pane will have gone.'
Frank Richards

My schoolmate, a Chinese named Wah,
Says 'l' when he ought to say 'r'.
To avoid asking the plice
Of a plate of flied lice,
He orders instead caviare.
Anon

A young person of Tomahawk Bluff
Carried pistols to make him look tough.
When they asked, 'Do you chew?'
He replied, 'Yes I do
I'm a wegular wetch of a wough.'
Anon

There was a young lady named Psyche
Was heard to ejaculate 'Pcryche!'
For, when riding her pbych
She ran over a ptych
And fell over some rails that were pspyche.

Anon

The Reverend W. A. Spooner,
Nailed sorth in a schee-masted throoner
When he reached the Porth Nole
He exclaimed, 'Sess my bloul!
The scandlape is all leak and blunar.'

Anon

There was a young lady named Menzies*
Who said, 'Do you know what this thinzies?'
Said her aunt, with a gasp
'Why my dear, that's a wasp!
And you're holding the end where the stinzies.

Anon

* *pronounced Min-gis*

A gent with a drooping moustache
Chewed some hair out while eating his hache.
The phrases profane
That he shrieked in his pain,
We shall represent here with a dache.

Anon

An odd couple living in Gloucester
Had a beautiful daughter but loucester.
She fell from a yacht,
And never the spot
Could be found where the cold waves had toucester.
Janet Rogers

There was an old man on a yacht
Who was trying to tie a reef nacht.
He said, 'It's uncanny
How it turns out a granny;
I'll study it up in *Whacht's Whacht*.'
Anon

A Welshman who went to Strathpeffer
Was struck in the back by a heffer;
He merely said, 'Ow
What a nasty rude cow!
The Scotch have no manners whateffer.'
Anon

There was an old man of Hawaii
Who ate too much whale and egg paii,
So quaffing some sperm oil
He quitted life's turmoil
Without even saying 'Goodbaii'.
Anon

A short-sighted Russian called Bakesti,
One day made a dreadful mistakeski,
He thought a brown bear
(Fast asleep) was a chair,
But discovered his mistakeski too lateski!

Patricia Merrien

Miss Minnie McFinney of Bute
Fed always, and only, on frutte.
Said she, 'Let the coarse
Eat of beef and of horse,
I'm a peach, and that's all there is tutte.'

Anon

An old man from the town and his daughter
Tumbled into choppy sea water.
Said the man, looking grim,
'Neither of us can swim
How I wish someone'd tortoise or taughter!'
Anon

There was a young lady from Reims,
Who it seims had bad nightmares and dreims,
Just before dawn
She'd walk on the lawn
And awake in the streim with loud screims.
Michelle Morris

There was a kind curate of Kew
Who kept a large cat in each pew,
Where he taught it each week
Alphabetical Greek,
But it never got further than *Mu*
Anon

Said an earnest young fellow of Tetuan,
'Oh, don't let my new puppy PetuAnn
He's a dear little chap
But if on your lap
He remains, I'm afraid he will wetuAnn.'
Langford Reed

Last night – such a scene in the House,
The member for Slopton-on-Slouse
Called the member for Herm
A despicable worm,
Who retorted by shouting, 'You louse.'
Langford Reed

A railway official at Crewe
Met an engine one day that he knew.
Tho' he smiled and he bowed,
The engine was proud.
It cut him – it cut him in two.
Anon

A gourmet who came from Nevada,
Had a simply remarkable lada,
His puddings were rowly,
His ravioli unholy,
And you should try his hot enchilada!
Michelle Morris

LIMERICKS WITH A DIFFERENCE

To end with, here are some limericks with an added twist – they are all written in prose!

Dear Mam
I am larning to spel I hoap
you an dad are boath well this
skool is kwite nice but Ive run
away twyss
With luv from your dorter
yung Nell
Cyril Bibby

Dear Pater,
(And Mater, and Kid), please
could you send me ten quid? My
tuckshop account requires that
amount to clear it.
Yours hopefully, Syd
Cyril Bibby

The train that was due to depart at 8.10 is not likely to start. We're working to rule: you'd best get a mule or a bike or a horse and a cart.
Cyril Bibby

All flights that are leaving today may well be hi-jacked on the way - but don't lose your nerve, for we shall still serve a pleasant cold meal on a tray.
Cyril Bibby

Try writing some of your own – it's good fun!

ACKNOWLEDGEMENTS

A book like this is enormous fun to put together especially as all sorts of people pitch in and offer suggestions and help. I would like to thank the following in particular: Liz Bland, Lisa Buchan, Aubrey Howard, Cyril Fletcher (for generously yielding up his chance of fame), Diana Newlands, Mike Petty, the Reverend John Prior, David Pollock, Lyneth Salisbury, Hetty Wallace, with special thanks to Christina Barnes, Deborah Bourne and Nick Wetton for their expert advice. Last, but not least, I would like to thank my family without whom none of this would have been possible.

I should like to thank the following for their generosity in allowing me to reproduce their limericks in this volume: Janet Allen; Judy Allen; Dr Cyril Bibby; Ian Botham; Joan G. Brown; Max Bygraves; Simon Cann; East Moseley Junior School, Coventry; Charlie Chester; Arthur Cox; Leslie Crowther; Wendy Cope for her limerick taken from *Sweet and Sour* edited by Christopher Logue (Batsford 1983); Kenny Everett; Barry Fantoni; Andrew Jones; Dr David Hatch, The Hospital for Sick Children, Great Ormond Street, London; Emma Henderson; Don Howe; Valerie Hudson; Miles Kington; John Letts for Limericks from *A Little Treasury of Limericks Fair and Foul* (Pan, 1973); T.L. McCarthy; Spike Milligan for limericks from *Silly Verse for Kids* (Dobson, 1969) and *101 Best and Only Limericks of Spike Milligan* (Sphere 1982); Bob Monkhouse; Michelle Morris; Richard Murdoch; Alastair, Diana and Gordon Newlands; Michael Palin for limericks from *Limericks* (Hutchinson's Children's Books Ltd, 1985); E.O. Parrott for his limerick published in *Limerick Delight* (Puffin, 1985); Paul Rand; Frank Richards; Dyan Sheldon; Jackie Shorey; Paul Sidey; Ruth Spencer; Eric Sykes; Ida Thurtle; Marguerite Varday for her limerick 'Strange Tastes' from *Stuff and Nonsense* edited by Michael Dugan (William Collins Pty. Ltd. Copyright, Marguerite Varday 1980.); Colin West; David Woodsford.

Several of these contributors have donated their fee to St Thomas Hospital, London.

I should also like to thank the following: Mrs Joan Langford Reed for permission to reproduce all limericks by her father Langford Reed and for the limericks from *The Complete Limerick Book* (Jarrolds, 1924) and *The Indiscreet Limerick Book* (Jarrolds, 1928); Mrs Jean Harrowven for limericks by R. Crisp, E.R. Franklin, Malcolm Farrow, F.O. Brewster, Pamela Murphy, Margaret Clarke, C. Carter, Julie Ling and R. Saunders from her book, *The Limerick Makers* (Research Publishing Company, 1976); Batsford Ltd for limericks from *Sweet and Sour*, edited Christopher Logue (1983); Century Hutchinson Ltd for limericks from *Janet Roger's Crazy Limericks* (Arrow Books, 1984) and the limerick by Colin West from *A Step in the Wrong Direction*, (Hutchinson, 1985); J.M. Dent and Sons Ltd for the limerick by Margaret Mahy from *Nonstop Nonsense* (1977); Faber and Faber for limericks from *Verse and Worse*, edited by Arnold Silcock; Gale Research Company, Detroit, for limericks reprinted from *Carolyn Wells Book of American Limericks* (originally published 1925, republished by Tower Books, Book Tower, Detroit, 1972); A.M. Heath and Company for the limerick by Conrad Aitken; grateful acknowledgement to Macmillan Publishing Co., New York, for limericks from *An Explosion of Limericks* edited by Vyvyan Holland. Copyright C. Cassell and Co. Ltd, 1967. Peter Pauper Press for limericks from *The World's Best Limericks* (1951); for 17 limericks from *Punch* magazine, reproduced by permission of *Punch*.

Every effort has been made to trace copyright holders. We would be grateful to hear from any copyright holders not here acknowledged.

Doctor, Doctor £1.50
Compiled by Peter Eldin
Illustrated by Kate Shannon

Doctor, Doctor, I feel like a dog.
Well, sit down and tell me about it.
I'm not allowed on the furniture.

Doctor: Take four teaspoonfuls of this medicine before every meal.
Patient: But we've only got three teaspoons!

Doctor, Doctor, I feel like a pair of curtains.
Well, pull yourself together.

Split your sides laughing at these rib-tickling jokes which are sure to give you and your friends a real tonic. A joke a day will keep the doctor away, and here are 96 cram-packed pages from the Kind of the Jokers, Peter Eldin.

From medicines to maniacs, from lost memories to lost mouth organs, and from mystery diseases to melting plastic surgeons, DOCTOR, DOCTOR is full of medical mirth which will have you in stitches. And laughter is the best medicine – just what the doctor ordered!

A Piccolo Original

Peter Eldin
Who's Zoo £1.25

A collection of jungle jokes and riddles

What thlithers along the ground and goeth hith?
A snake with a lisp!

Where do cows go on holiday?
Moo York!

What does a budgerigar get when it goes to the doctor?
Tweetment!

Who's Zoo? is a comic collection of jolly jestful, jungle jocularity just guaranteed to make chimps chortle, snakes snicker, camels cackle, tigers tittle and hyenas howl with hilarity . . .

From mirthful mammoths to feathered funsters there's a horse laugh on every page in this bumper bundle of beastly buffoonery . . .

Find out why humming birds hum, what keys will not open locks, who is Tarzan's favourite singer, where do you take a sick horse and what's the difference between a camel and a flea . . .

A Piccolo Original

The Piccolo Bumper Puzzle Book 1 £1.95
Edited by Mike Grimshaw

Crosswords . . . Mazes . . . Name the Faces . . . Picture Crosswords . . . Here is a pretty perplexing colossal collection of tantalising teasers, both verbal and visual, to baffle your brain in the car or the train, at home or on holiday, on the boat or the plane . . .

A Piccolo Original

compiled by Robin Burgess
The Piccolo Bumper Crossword Book: 1

More than 600,000 young crossword fanatics have enjoyed *Piccolo Crossword Books*. Now we have gathered 200 of the very best puzzles into one bumper volume for hours and hours of puzzling pleasure!

compiled by Robin Burgess
The Piccolo Bumper Crossword Book: 2

Improve your word power! Increase your vocabulary! Get the best introduction to the fascinating adult world of crossword puzzles!

Hundreds of thousands of young crossword fanatics have already enjoyed *Piccolo Crossword Books*. Now we have gathered 200 more of the very best puzzles into a second bumper volume to give you hours of fun and puzzling pleasure!

Carey Miller
A Dictionary of Monsters and Mysterious Beasts £1.95

A huge collection of the most extraordinary creatures ever to trample the earth. Here are monsters and mysterious beasts, foul and frightening, from the Boneless Bird of Paradise and the Two-Headed Amphisbaena to the Eight-Forked Serpent and the Wild Beast of Barriesdale. Some are real, some don't exist . . . or do they . . . ?

A Piccolo Original

Toni Arthur
Everyday Singaway £2.95

A marvellous collection of songs from many lands, *Everyday Singaway* has folk songs, work songs and play songs; joyful songs, tender songs, active songs and sad songs; traditional songs, unusual songs and much, much more!